40
COUNTRY

Compiled by

Stephen Chapman

Published by

York Railpress
16 Woodside Avenue
York YO3 0QS

ISBN 0 946371 00 8

Front cover: 40007 rumbles over Leven Viaduct, Ulverston, with a ballast train *(S. W. Robson)*.

This is Forty Country

A flock of bedraggled sheep seek what shelter they can from the Pennine drizzle behind a drystone wall. Only the cry of a solitary curlew and the gushing of a tumbling stream punctuate the still, damp atmosphere.

Within moments a dripping signal wire flexes itself and a distant white arm points towards the leaden sky – the only sign of movement on the railway which has penetrated these lonely parts for well over a century.

Then, the stillness becomes total, even the babbling stream is silenced, as if in anticipation of some great event – like the calm before the storm.

On a remote hillside a faint rumbling gradually draws closer, becoming more and more distinct until, with a thundering roar, a 133-ton monster rounds the bend into full view. The pounding of its 16 English Electric pistons becomes more intense as its wheels grind against the wet, blackened rails.

With a final thrust over the summit the power is shut off, leaving only the whistling of the fan, accompanied by the rumbling and rattling wagons following in its wake as it coasts into a cutting and out of sight.

Calm returns to the fells, the curlew calls again, the stream tumbles on its way and the signal clatters back to its forbidding 'on' position.

Could it be that everything on that fellside had stopped to witness the passage of 2,000 horses straining at the yoke – the equestrian equivalent of this powerful monster, the British Rail Class 40 diesel-electric locomotive.

Opposite: With the paint hardly dry a brand new D306 makes a travelling companion of a class K1 2-6-0 at Burn, en-route from York to Doncaster.

(E. Sanderson)

The heavy freight trains which have to be heaved over, round or through the Northern fells are still very much the domain of what are some of British Rail's oldest main-line diesel locomotives. Routes like the Diggle line between Huddersfield and Manchester; the Cumbrian coast line, with its estuaries noted for their fierce tides; and, of course, the Settle and Carlisle. These lines belong to the Forties – this is Forty Country.

Their versatility ensures, however, that the class is not confined just to freight work. Every summer delighted enthusiasts witness the return of the Forties to front-line passenger work as they take up such Saturday duties as Manchester-Scarborough, Newcastle-Blackpool and York-Llandudno trains. Throughout the year they still find regular employment on North Wales expresses, especially between Manchester, Bangor and Holyhead.

It seems strange to recall that when the first English Electric Type 4's, as they were known then, took to the rails nearly 25 years ago, five of the initial batch, Nos. D200/2-5,

Photo: E. Sanderson

were allocated to a London depot, Stratford, for work on the Liverpool Street-Norwich main line. The other five went to Finsbury Park from where they soon began to forge their first links with the north, working principal East Coast expresses, such as the 'Flying Scotsman', although at the time they did not match up to the A3 and A4 Pacifics which were being rebuilt with double chimneys and blastpipes.

The next batch, D210-35, went to the London Midland Region for work on the West Coast Main Line and trains to Manchester and Liverpool. They were given names of famous ocean liners which had sailed from Liverpool, thus linking them indisputedly with the North West.

Over the next few years new examples were delivered to York, Gateshead, Longsight, Edge Hill, Haymarket and other northern depots where the duties were varied, often unglamorous, but never menial. By the time deliveries of new locomotives had ceased in 1962 there were 200 of them pounding the rails from London to Inverness on both sides of the country.

Now their days are nearly done, but as scrappings become a regular feature it is likely that some 50 air-braked members of the class will see the next couple of years – they are simply indispensible.

During 1982 enthusiasts have travelled from all over Britain to Forty Country, be it Llandudno or York, Carlisle or Manchester, to see their favourites at work, and they have not been disappointed. We hope that the pictures which follow will bring back happy memories of days spent at the lineside or in the first coach, long after the Forties have gone the way of the Deltics and the Westerns.

The North West

Since their earliest days the whistling growl of the Class 40's has reverberated between the fells and mill chimneys of north west England.

With Manchester at the very heart of Forty Country, no less than 44 members of the class are, at the time of writing, allocated to Longsight depot, many out-stationed at sub-depots such as Guide Bridge, Newton Heath and Northwich.

Their duties are mainly freight but include nightly convoys of newspaper trains, ensuring that the Northern editions reach breakfast tables on both sides of the Pennines. Another 23 are at Springs Branch, Wigan, often working coal trains from the Lancashire pits while Carlisle and its large marshalling yard has twelve.

The Forties can be found on almost any kind of train on any line from Cheshire to Cumbria but a special mention should be made of their exploits on the Manchester-North Wales expresses, for which they have become justly famous.

Green Class 40 No. 40106 at Manchester Victoria with a train from Bangor on 28.8.82. *(Stephen Chapman)*

40182 heads empty ballast wagons for Bayston Hill quarry through Shrewsbury on 14.9.81. *(Brian Morrison)*

Above: 40084 races the 09.26 Newcastle-Blackpool through Kearsley, between Manchester and Bolton, on 28.8.82.

Below: 40121 crosses the famous Chat Moss with the 13.53 Llandudno-York on the same day. *(Both Stephen Chapman)*

40182 heads a ballast train through Helsby, on the edge of the Wirral, on 18.9.81. *(Brian Morrison)*

Above: Green-liveried 40106 ambles a train of empty news vans through Manchester Victoria on 2.10.82.

Below: 40184 about to head the 09.45 from Manchester Victoria to Bangor on 7.8.82. *(Both Stephen Chapman)*

Above: Early morning mist lifts to reveal the 09.00 Blackpool-Newcastle drifting through Bolton behind 40079 on 28.8.82.

Below: 40004 at Guide Bridge after working a summer Saturday Skegness-Manchester train on 21.8.82.

(Both Stephen Chapman)

Settle and Carlisle Whistlers: Above 40169 thunders through Dent with a northbound train of ICI tanks on 20.7.82 while, below, 40148 is seen near Ais Gill on the same day with a Carlisle-Healey Mills freight.

(Both Stephen Chapman)

Above: 40063 rumbles over Ravenglass viaduct on a Cumbrian coast freight on 25.8.82.

Below: 40141 rolls an up tank train into Carnforth on 25.8.82.

(Both Stephen Chapman)

North Wales

The North Wales main line deserves a special place in the Class 40 story. After a long association with the class it has now become the last bastion of regular Class 40 passenger haulage as they dash to and fro with expresses from Manchester and Crewe.

On summer Saturdays the Forties have been regular and sturdy workers on a variety of holiday trains. Most notably those between York, Leeds and Llandudno.

In addition they work a large proportion of freight and ballast trains along the route, often from their stabling point at Llandudno Junction.

With all this activity, it is easy to see why the North Wales line receives many visitors each summer for the sake of its trains rather than its beaches. As a result, Forty fans will no doubt be well aquainted with many of the scenes in this section.

40184 brings the 13.58 Bangor-Manchester into Llandudno Junction on 7.8.82. *(Stephen Chapman)*

Above: 40128 snakes along the bank of the Conwy estuary as it nears Llandudno Junction with the 13.53 Llandudno-York on 7.8.82.

Below: 40192 storms the 10.45 Manchester Victoria-Holyhead through the castle wall at Conwy, also on 7.8.82. *(Both Stephen Chapman)*

Above: Rolling the 15.17 Holyhead-Manchester along the sea front at Colwyn Bay on 7.8.82 was 40192.

Below: 40063 approaching Colwyn Bay with a train from Crewe, also on 7.8.82. *(Both Stephen Chapman)*

Llandudno Junction's tall, lean signalbox watches over 40184 as it rolls the 13.58 Bangor-Manchester into the station on 7.8.82. *(Stephen Chapman)*

Over Diggle

The Diggle route across the Pennines has long been a Class 40 stamping ground. Right up to the mid-1970's they regularly hauled Liverpool-Newcastle expresses, sharing them with Gateshead 'Peaks'. Even today, although very much a Class 47 route so far as passenger work is concerned, it still sees the odd 40-hauled Scarborough-Liverpool Inter-City.

As ever, they are still to be seen on freight turns but it is on summer Saturdays when they come into their own. The Diggle route forms the central core of the holiday route between main centres of population and the east and west coast resorts. On these days enthusiasts at Diggle are delighted by the sight and sound of a steady procession of 'Whistlers' as they hammer to and fro on Newcastle-Blackpool, Manchester-Scarborough and York-Llandudno trains amid delightful scenery.

This section of photos, by Stephen Chapman, preserves for ever the excitement of a summer Saturday on the Diggle route.

40184 thrashes towards the summit at Diggle with the 09.00 Llandudno-York on 12.6.82.

Gliding over Saddleworth Viaduct with the 09.00 York-Llandudno on 12.6.82 was 40050.

Above: 40124 is dwarfed by her Pennine surroundings as she approaches Standedge Tunnel at Marsden with the 07.52 Leeds-Llandudno on 21.8.82.

Below: Emerging from Standedge Tunnel on the same day was 40184 with the 08.40 Manchester-Scarborough.

Above: Excitement at Huddersfield as 40136 arrives with the 08.40 Manchester-Scarborough on 12.6.82.

Below: The 'Anglian Whistler' railtour passing Gledholt behind 40012 'Aureol' and 40081 on 1.5.82.

Yorkshire

Today the Yorkshire home of the Class 40's is Healey Mills, the large Wakefield marshalling yard. From there they work a succession of freight trains in all directions: westward to Manchester and Preston, northwards to Carlisle and the North East, and south and eastwards to Humberside, Lincolnshire and even their original home, East Anglia.

At busy times in the summer the 'HM' Forties are turned out for passenger duty on a host of seaside specials. One of their most regular turns has been the mid-week and Sunday Wakefield-Scarborough round trip, as well as sharing the Blackpool and Llandudno runs with their foreign sisters.

In this section we take a look at the class at work in Yorkshire, covering an area from industrial Sheffield to historic York, and from Doncaster to Skipton, gateway to the Dales.

Below: 40185 moves freight through a deserted Wakefield Kirkgate in the direction of Healey Mills on 30.6.82. *(Stephen Chapman)*

Above: A train of Presflo cement wagons is hauled through Shipley by 40047 on 19.5.81.

Below: 40086 waits at Skipton with the 12.50 Healey Mills-Carlisle freight on 25.5.81. *(Both Stephen Chapman)*

A wintery scene at Crimple Tunnel, near Harrogate, in the early 1960's as D255 heads a Liverpool-Newcastle express via the Wetherby and Ripon lines. *(E. Sanderson)*

Above: 40148 heads the 08.40 Manchester-Scarborough over the River Ouse and away from York on 6.6.81.

Below: 40169 brings the 07.52 Leeds-Llandudno into Dewsbury on 12.6.82. *(Both Stephen Chapman)*

Above: 40006 climbing Micklefield bank with the 17.00 Scarborough-Liverpool on 28.7.82.

Below: 40025 'Lucitania' leaves Doncaster with the Muir of Ord grain train on 20.8.82. *(Both Stephen Chapman)*

Above: 40081 nears York with the Sunday 08.35 Wakefield-Scarborough on 29.8.82 while (below) 40185 heads the 09.00 York-Llandudno in the opposite direction on 3.7.82. *(Both Stephen Chapman)*

North Eastern

At the time of writing only a handful of Forties remain allocated to Gateshead depot, once the home of many, and none to Thornaby.

Nevertheless, they are certainly far from finished in the North East, working as they do a nightly procession of Speedlink freight, and sometimes East Coast Main Line passenger trains through the area.

As with many other areas, the class see work on summer Saturday extras and in the North East they have been regulars on Newcastle-Blackpool and Glasgow-Scarborough trains.

Whilst they are much thinner on the ground in the North East nowadays, the Forties can still reward the photographer who waits patiently by the great bridges across the Tyne and the Tweed, or at the top of the Norman keep which towers above Newcastle's Central Station.

Split-headcode 40131 waits at Scarborough with the 18.58 for Wakefield on 25.7.82. *(Stephen Chapman)*

40061 takes the empty stock of the 09.00 from Blackpool out of Newcastle Central and away to Heaton carriage sidings on 14.8.82. *(Stephen Chapman)*

Scarborough line Forties: above, 40002 heads the 19.02 Scarborough-Manchester along the Scarborough-York line on Sunday 15.8.82 while, below, 40131 hammers the 18.50 Scarborough-Wakefield through Haxby on 27.7.82. *(Both Stephen Chapman)*

40001 rolls through Carrbridge with an up freight on 31.5.77.

Crewe

Lurking in the depths of the diesel depot on 22.5.82 were 40190 and 40030 'Scythia'. *(Stephen Chapman)*

Above: 40160 with an up train of empty news vans on 22.5.82 and, on the same day (below), 40131 receiving attention at the diesel depot.
(Both Stephen Chapman)

40155 waits in Platform 9 with the 19.02 Scarborough-Manchester on 25.7.82. *(Stephen Chapman)*

Above: Heading south from York Station with the Newcastle-Manchester (Red Bank) empty news vans.
Below: 40138 hauls a tamper into York Yard South on 14.9.81.
(Both Stephen Chapman)

Old Haunts

Above: Almost new, D202 races the 15.45 Norwich-Liverpool Street through Bethnal Green on 6.8.58.

Below: D207 climbs Holloway Bank out of King's Cross with the down 'Flying Scotsman' on 7.10.58. *(Both Brian Morrison)*

D293 is serviced at Camden shed, London, between turns on the 'Merseyside Express' at the end of the 1950's.
(E. Sanderson)

Class 40 Allocation Details
(Summer 1982)

Manchester Longsight (LO):	40004/8/9/14/20/24/25/27/28/29/30/33/34/35/44/46/49/50/55/61/63/76/79/80/82/90/94/96/97/99/106/107/117/118/133/135/145/148/153/167/168/170/171/184
	Total: 44
Springs Branch, Wigan (SP):	40013/15/19/91/93/126/128/129/131/155/157/160/164/172/174/177/180/181/185/186/188/191/194
	Total: 23
Healey Mills (HM):	40003/6/47/52/56/68/69/73/74/77/81/86/92/104/121/161/169/183/192/195/196/197
	Total: 22
Carlisle (KD):	40001/2/12/22/60/62/65/101/138/150/158/162
	Total: 12
Gateshead (GD):	40007/57/58/84/85/124/152/198
	Total: 8
	Grand Total: 109

NB: Like most British Rail main line locomotives, Class 40's are not bound to the areas around their home depots. For example, there is nothing to prevent a Gateshead '40' turning up on a Holyhead-Manchester train or a Longsight '40' in Scotland.

Principal Class 40 Routes

Holyhead/Bangor-Manchester/Crewe	P/F
Crewe-Shrewsbury-Chester	F
Manchester/Guide Bridge-Northwich/Chester/ Birkenhead	F
Manchester/Wigan-Liverpool	F
Manchester-Preston-Blackpool	P/F/N
Manchester-Sheffield-Grimsby	N
Manchester/Guide Bridge-Buxton/Chinley	F
Manchester-Newcastle	N
Manchester-Skegness/Yarmouth	P*
Healey Mills-Manchester/Preston	F
Preston-Blackburn-Hellifield-Carlisle	F
Healey Mills-Skipton-Carlisle/Carnforth	F
Carnforth-Barrow-Workington	F
Healey Mills-Goole/Hull	F
Healey Mills-Scunthorpe/March	F
Healey Mills-York-Tyne	F
Peterborough-Doncaster-Newcastle-Edinburgh-Aberdeen/Inverness	P*/F
Aberdeen-Perth-Glasgow	P/F
Carlisle-Dumfries-Glasgow	F
Wakefield Westgate-Scarborough	P*
Manchester Victoria-Scarborough	P*
York/Leeds-Llandudno	P*
Newcastle-Blackpool	P*

P: Passenger
F: Freight
N: News
* Summer service only

Photographs in this book by:-

Stephen Chapman
Brian Morrison
S. W. Robson
E. Sanderson

Back cover: *Stephen Chapman*

Phototypeset & Printed by Wood & Richardson Ltd., King's Square, York